ME AND HER SHADOW

poems by

Christine R. Lund

Finishing Line Press
Georgetown, Kentucky

ME AND HER SHADOW

For Kaja Mauldin
1978-2001

Christine and Kaja, 1996 high school graduation

Copyright © 2020 by Christine Lund
ISBN 978-1-64662-327-3 First Edition
All rights reserved under International and Pan-American Copyright Conventions.
No part of this book may be reproduced in any manner whatsoever without written
permission from the publisher, except in the case of brief quotations embodied in
critical articles and reviews.

Publisher: Leah Huete de Maines
Editor: Christen Kincaid
Cover Art: Photograph by Neil C. Trager, Drawing by Kaja Mauldin
Interior Art: Photograph by Neil C. Trager, Drawing by Kaja Mauldin
Dedication Photo: Bill Mauldin
Author Photo: Neil C. Trager
Cover Design: Elizabeth Maines McCleavy

Order online: www.finishinglinepress.com
also available on amazon.com

Author inquiries and mail orders:
Finishing Line Press
P. O. Box 1626
Georgetown, Kentucky 40324
U. S. A.

Table of Contents

OVERTURE
The Sacrifice of Isaac 1

ACT I – ANGRY ANGELS
Me and Her Shadow 2
My Friendly Night Lights 3
Angry Angels 4
After a Concert 5
Castle 6
Rainbow Pencils 7
All Souls' Day 8
Pumpkin 9
Hostages to Fate 10
Gibbous Moon 11
After the Mushroom Cloud 12
Quivering Light 13
Celebration 14
Visitation 15
A Rarity 16
The Red Tulips 18

ACT II – THE CROW AND THE BUTTERFLY
The Crow and the Butterfly 19
Day of the Dead 20
Soul Journeys 21
After Life 22
Approaching Candles in the Dark 23
Chagall Kiss Cup 24
Face to Face 25
Coffee Stains 26
Some Visitations 27
The Girl in the Grave 28
Guiding Lights 29
Becoming a Healer 30
Her Bag of Tricks 31
My Private Muse 32
As If I Could Fly 33
Night Vision 34

FINALE
Roll the Credits 35

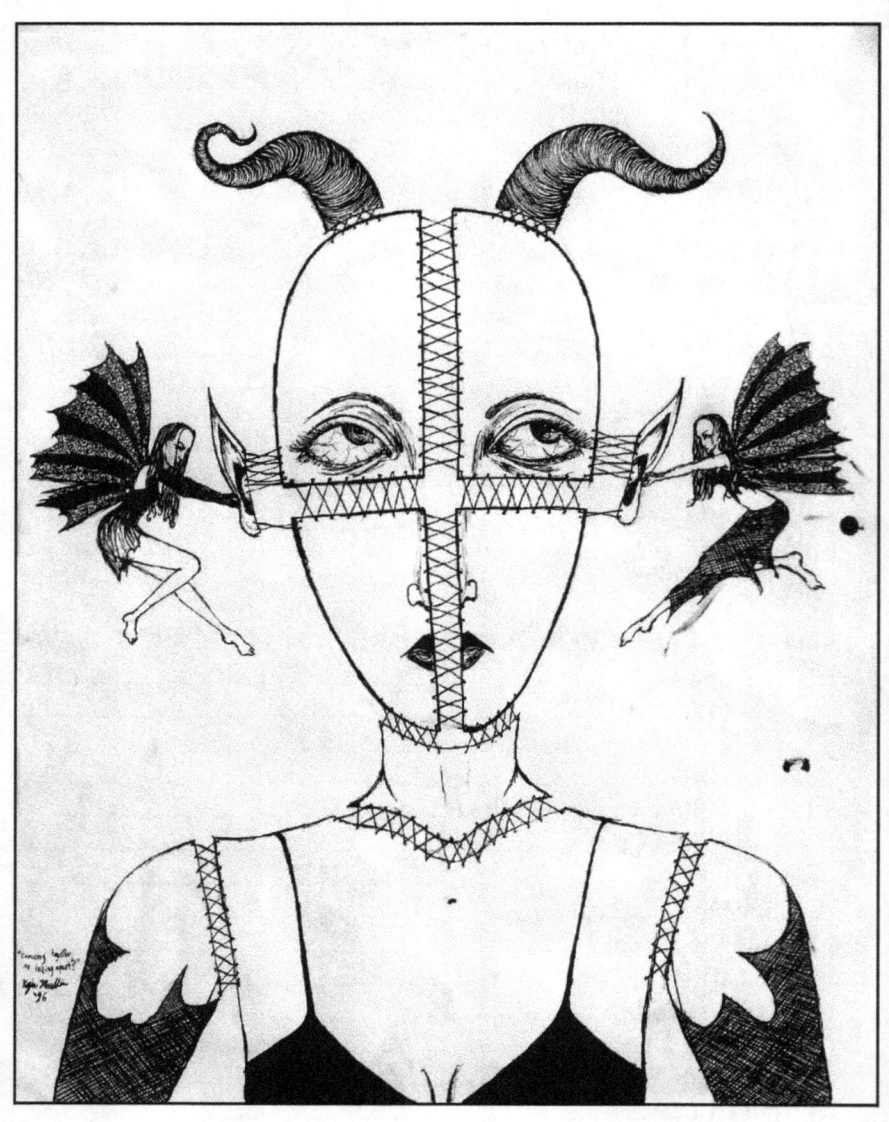

OVERTURE

The Sacrifice of Isaac
   (Revised Non-Standard Version)

I told my child,
you have to let her go.
If you love her,
you will know
when you let the kitty
do what she wants,
go where she
wants to go.
As you open
and empty your arms,
as you watch
that one go,
it's love.

ACT ONE: ANGRY ANGELS

Me and Her Shadow

Will I intuit, how to name
the process I am in,
its shape—I know its genesis,
and that I have been taking
many steps, day by day
along my private path,
and finding gifts along the way.
New friends, and a partnership—
sources of strength and solace.
Joy and beauty lift me from
the sorrow that lines my soul,
covers it like a fitted sheet
that feels like home.
It's welcoming, always with me.
I am not journeying away,
from the experience of her death.
Rather, I am taking her with me,
wherever I grow—so, come along
with me and her shadow, dancing
onward, to these songs.

My Friendly Night Lights

I snuck and took one last look at Venus on the half shell—
No! Venus, the planet, riding through the sky, with the crescent moon.
I'm not at the Uffizi, nor looking at the Goddess,
by Botticelli, in a book,
but, looking out the window of my husband's studio—
a room that many years ago, belonged to my daughter,
when she was alive. She was last there 18 years ago,
busy fighting cancer, at this time of year—it had returned,
after she finished treatments, with chemo and radiation.
The signs were not good, and later she succumbed to it
or rather, it overtook her—my conscious brain did not recall
that the end of February was the turning point, but my heart
became disrupted. While discussing the anniversary effect
of childbirth with a friend, my experience with the other end
came back, the opposite of birth,
that most mothers don't have—

I am the exception, rather than the rule, thank goodness,
or our species would not be doing too well, but headed
for extinction—something I didn't mean to ponder, just that
what happened to me and my child is rare. It's like an exotic flower,
a poisonous one, such as the Venus fly trap in a movie she liked,
Little Shop of Horrors, which brings us back to the Goddess
of love, up in the sky, and depicted in paintings and sculptures.
I have studied, and embody that archetype,
and other ones, like Demeter—
I dove into psychology through myths and metaphors, a twist
to help me understand the plight of women, living in the patriarchy
as second class citizens, fighting for wholeness and independence.
I dove in fully, with my daughter back inside me—this time I host
her visiting soul, not a growing body—
she lends me extra strength, and her
idiosyncratic moxie—the eyes to notice Venus,
with the crescent moon, rising.

Angry Angels

Dear Kaja,
I went to a folk market fair
and met you in an artifact there.
Artists from around the globe had gathered
to demonstrate crafts from home.
Bright beads from South Africa
drew me into a booth, and I could not pass
a beaded white angel ornament,
with an angry expression on her brow.
I looked around, and considered the rest,
left the booth, but I had to come back
and buy the angry angel.

I thought perhaps I'd give her up
as a present, to my mother or a friend
but I find I want to keep her for myself,
this piece of my angry angel.
How are you doing, and where do you roam
Sweet spirit, are you looking down?
I have a new love; your brother has grown.
But there's always room in my heart
for this song to you, my angry angel.
I wish you peace, dear, angry angel.

After a Concert

It seemed indulgent
to go to a film and concert—the premiere,
by and about a musician I know, or knew
back at a formative time, when my daughter
was friends with his step daughter.
But, my brother offered to take me
as a birthday present, so it seemed justified
and we went, and enjoyed it.

It was a time when the kids were innocent
decades ago, and a melody he played
brought it all back, as music can do.
My emotions were activated, not in some
pointless nostalgia—rather, my heart
became an arrow shooting back to when
now looked like a hopeful future, for
at least our children—I couldn't have predicted it.

I have not been recently in touch
with his wife, who is my friend.
And, it's understandable that life moves on
especially when a link was lost, with
my daughter's death—the girls might have stayed in contact.
As the musician said, about the death of colleagues,
that's the problem with living so long
Not everyone is so lucky—but, we celebrate our lives.

He was gracious, and grateful for the gift of time.
I am also, despite the shadow side—
the other shoe that dropped, and just lies there.
Once more, I find another day before me
with dry heat, and birdsong—he played another tune
about rain falling, and said, we need some here.
May I also stay attuned to Earth and her pains
and glories—she, who accepts and understands my story.

Castle

I was thinking about the early 1980's
when I heard a strange sound—
I had to turn around to see
what had just passed me, in the arroyo.
I saw the back of a bicyclist—
he had found a path, through chamisa bushes.
Satisfied, my mind went back
to memories of young motherhood.
I went back to catch a thread,
for the daughter of a friend.
It led me to her toy castle, that she gave
to my toddler daughter, now gone,
complete with little people—
led me to a time with her
that was dormant
and now, briefly, back.
The object for the experience I felt—
objective correlative, I think it's called.
I am thankful, for that
a feather touch
of tenderness.

Rainbow Pencils

My husband found—lost to memory!
in the garage, a tube container
hand painted by my daughter—
a yellow sun with rays, that took some skill—
so, she was not a young child then.
Inside, there was a stash
of rainbow colored pencils.
They were not yet sharpened, and each one
moved from blue to yellow to red, and back—
Green, orange and purple are just hints
at the borders—they shine brightly in the light,
and on each one, printed in white,
her name is stamped.
Eraser is also white—the lead is black
and the eraser works!
The colors are luminous.
You found them at a time, when our yellow pencils
were being used up—I wear them to the nub.
You brought one to me, and said, here are some
new ones—my heart rose in delight.
I clapped my hands and then, sharpened one,
as if it were a gift from beyond—
Something that had been there for me, all along,
like Dorothy and the ruby slippers,
from a story she had loved,
sort of like a magic wand.
She collected those, also—a torch
to be passed, arrived, at just the right moment.

All Souls' Day

Back to Standard Time
The standard,
but there's less of it, now
than daylight savings,
due to a change in the law.
Don't let me start in—
I don't mind the extra hour
in fact, I relish it.

Images appear
like photos in developing trays,
old technology—
A spirit may whisper
Light seen through wind in trees
shimmers on bookends
piled high by my writing seat—

Openness to what, the spirit perceives
What door may blow ajar,
twixt them and me.
What message wafting in
What blockage, eased—
Let me reiterate.
Welcome, please be.

Pumpkin

I brought a pumpkin to you
on the Day of the Dead.
The holiday always was a favorite of yours.
One year, you made small altars
in our dining room,
to ancestors—
my father
and your father's wife before me,
not distinguishing
precise lineage.
Young hearts don't discriminate—
at least, yours never did.
You also liked to dress up
on Halloween,
the costumes more elaborate
each year through your teens, and
beyond—I can't recall your last one.
In 2000, were you well enough?
No matter; I remember you,
and find it ironic that
you, who honored those gone before
are with them now,
though prematurely—
in the same ground,
now topped with a seasonal pumpkin.

Hostages to Fate

When he was arguing
against having children, with me—
(After all, he had some
with the two wives before me)
My husband said, because then, you have
hostages to Fate.
Recently, that phrase
came back into my consciousness
In retrospect, I have to say
I see what he meant.
From the vantage point
of having won the argument,
which led to our two children—
a daughter, then a son
and my life as a mother,
which goes on and on,
in suffering, and in joy.
And, I still have my son—
the source of deep fulfillment
identity and fun.
So yes, it is all worth it
I would still
tell anyone.

Gibbous Moon

The day I saw my daughter's head
in the waxing, Gibbous moon,
it was still daylight in the arroyo
far into December, on the march to the Solstice.

As a young woman, she was bald several times.
At first, by choice, and later from medical treatments.
That is how she looked, when she died.

It was the oval shape, and the dark places
that look like facial features—
You took several photographs of the moon rise
as I gazed, again and again.

Hello and good-bye—always has it been,
in the light from our eyes, seeking what we have lost,
like a gift in the night—here for a while, then gone.

After the Mushroom Cloud

I caught a notion floating through my consciousness—
my daughter's death, and the aftermath
as a focus for my life's work since then.
I had a dual reaction
First, it seemed to ring true—
I was on to something.
Then, I noticed disappointment
Really? After all that has happened
inside my spirit since,
am I still defined and limited
by that seminal experience?
Actually, it was this morning
when I dared to say it,
when I sat quietly, not knowing
how to understand it, waiting.
And the word that surfaced
was anger.
I could feel the resentment
as part of the whole—
I had value, before that horror
landed like a bomb,
with the subsequent mushroom cloud.
My fury at it all lives on,
I guess, is what I found.
Just as cancer wracked her body,
my world view was wasted
I've been feeling my way ever since
through the fall out, shaken.

Quivering Light

I didn't mean to rend my flesh,
to prick my thumb with a thorn
from our dying roses, as I tossed them out.
I didn't mean to bruise my arm
either, but I did, by taking an impulsive
action—they had been so beautiful.
I was sad to notice they were drooping,
but still on our table, so I acted—

Out of sight, but never out of my heart,
this sadness from a deeper well.
Fifteen years ago this date,
I lost my daughter.
There; I've said it, as a tear descends
down my cheek to my upper lip.
Yesterday, after I voted early
I had the thought, now if I die
at least I voted, and then, I was confused—

No; I have to live longer
but it was a whisper, of what was ahead,
this day of remembrance
of when she was wrenched
away from this Earth
where my feet still tread—
where inside my heart,
her essence still lives.

Celebration

This used to be a busy day for me,
when she was growing up.
We always had a party for her
with friends and cake—
Her father used to let the kids
drive his riding mower,
or was it his old Army jeep, or both?
Down the dirt road, next to our house,
he put the gear in granny,
so it crawled along.
I think he walked next to it,
hand on the steering wheel
I was back at the house
feeling nervous.
We had champagne for the parents
who came to pick their kids up,
along with the cake.
Usually, the weather was nice
despite the volatility of Spring here,
and we could go outside.
I feel gratitude for the good times
that have happened
still present in my heart.
Love never dies, unlike our bodies
which go, as hers did, too young—
Happy birthday, dear Kaja,
I remember you with love.

Visitation

At the ready—incomplete
Lady waits, perhaps she'll read
try again that novel, where she drifted off
God, when was that? Months ago
Working always—office, home
news gathering, still, even though
election season's come and gone.

Unusual to rest and stretch
imagination; not be taken
by bad thoughts, disguising a haunting
of my favorite painful ghost.
I run away, but she is in my feet, and haste—
rapid heartbeat changes just the pace.
Like a treadmill, getting nowhere
till it hurts, and I am stopped.

Resting, and my child returns.
Perhaps I'll even notice her
but sometimes I do not.
I mean, why should I still be crushed
and have to wrench myself apart,
and see the mess and devastation
in there, that her death created?
She is my daughter, after all.
I never will be moving on,
no matter how I skate above
in fancy pirouettes—she comes.

I wince, as I recall the song
and sing its every note;
snap back to my daily chores,
puffy eyed, with thickened throat.
Let me journey back and forth
more gracefully, or not.
I am all the moments—seeking peace—
escaping—caught.

A Rarity

Sequences happen
Energy is released, through open channels
once blocked—now, they breathe
My body relaxes into who I can be.
I walked yesterday,
after the flooding rain passed through
our arroyo, in the warm light of day.
We saw the high water mark
darkening the banks.
Debris had piled up where we enter
the arroyo, obscuring our path
I couldn't identify what it was made of
We stepped over it, and walked on—
on our way, to discover more.

I don't recall ever seeing so many monarchs
flying in pairs, alone, in groups
Amazingly
resting on the ground
that was so wet, it looked like clay—
I had never seen butterflies there, before.
I asked you later, were there nutrients
in the wet soil, the sand—
you thought maybe it was the moisture
that attracted them.

A riot of butterflies
graced us on that walk,
so rare here, who knows when it may recur,
if ever, so I had to pause
before life moves along
and build this small altar—
This memory of a magical hour
I shared with you, and all life—all energy
flying through the arroyo—birds and dragonflies
as well as her animal totem—

a favorite type of butterfly
of my lost girl.
Such an abundance
of little orange monarchs,
that I thank the divine, for elusive spirits.

The Red Tulips

Tulips were blooming
when she came home to die
on May 1, 2001.
We took her picture
as she bent down, and smiled
to touch red petals
and inhale the aroma,
if any she was able to find.
I have the photograph
but not the child—
just a memory
to dampen my eyes.
Pain that lets me know,
my heart is alive.
Poised to break, again—
again, tulip time.

ACT TWO: THE CROW AND THE BUTTERFLY

The Crow and the Butterfly

A crow caws, flying by.
Butterflies found me, before she even died.
A friend showered her, towards the end
with colorful paper images.
Then, taped them to the walls around our house
Fifteen years later, some of them are still installed.
Before she died, they sparked me to recall
her sixth grade graduation, when a teacher
in a tribute said, Kaja, you resemble
a butterfly; I had that read at her service
in a park; and ever since, each time
I see a monarch or other type of butterfly,
I feel my heart smile and am comforted,
convinced that it's her, visiting.

Years later, at a time when crows
were perched on a cottonwood tree in our yard
cawing loudly, blotting out our peace and quiet,
it occurred to me that Crow might be
her other side, the difficult teenager
she had been, rebelling against
me in particular, as she became herself.
Harsh challenges—the about face from childhood,
jarring me to my bones.
Might the crows not be
her sounding off, completing the picture—
wide winged predator, to complement
the fragile majesty of the butterfly.
She could be two animal spirits,
both capable, of flight.

Day of the Dead

I am a woman who has lost a child
and today is the Day of the Dead.
Today is the day to honor our loved ones
who have died, and been buried or scattered—
I really don't like, that this is reality
and my daughter was put into the ground.
I really don't like, that I can only remember her
and not touch her cheek or her brow.
How has it happened, I can't see her impish smile—
How have I managed, to go on, alive?
What can I give her, anymore?
The cold fact is, nothing is left to be done for her,
but to keep in my heart, her love—
or is it my love for her, that lives on inside of me?
No matter; the feeling is strong
and carries with it all of my openness.
The future is linked to this hope,
that love never vanishes, only is redirected
I honor her on this day, with every note
that sings in my heart—with this tribute.

Soul Journeys

Household sounds block out the radio
I think it's the hum of the refrigerator.

Look out the window—my eyes find Venus
One point of cheer, in the dark blue sky.

This morning, I thought of my friend
who visited here, from New Zealand
She rarely makes the trip back home—
Last time, it was when I had a broken elbow, and
my daughter was receiving radiation treatments.
We were both recovering in that window.

Windows are closed now, against the cold
First freeze came last week, while she was with us.

Fall colors on favorite trees fell on the ground
Brightness disappeared—the leaves turned brown.

How do I deal with disappointment
drifting in with the wind—let it go by?
I search the leaves, still on the trees,
but I don't think they will shine for me
anymore, this season—the timing of the cold snap
was egregious—beauty was snatched away.

Sixteen years ago, my elbow slowly healed
But, I regret to say, cancer returned, and took my girl.

Life is what we've got—I gave my friend
a pencil, with my daughter's name on it.

You had found a bunch of them in the garage
I'm writing with one of them, right now—

I also give them, occasionally, to special people
This time, as if I could give her, a trip to New Zealand.

After Life

Silent raven flew overhead
off in the distance, just after I said,
Do you remember the song?
You answered that you did, "Something's Coming"
from *West Side Story*.
Her hospice nurse, named Bee
stood up at the memorial service,
and sang a few bars, said
my daughter was thinking of it,
knowing she would be dying soon,
as if death were an adventure
that she was looking forward to.

And now that I'm visiting
the ancient world of Avalon,
reading of it, largely because my daughter
was, in her last months—
I can't help but wonder,
if she took some hope in their belief
in reincarnation, though they didn't
call it by that name, but the Merlin said,
he'd been given a new life—and the Lady
of Avalon had a glimpse of her past one,
perceiving the death of another; so, I wonder
if it helped her, to meet her fate,
the ancients' concept that suffering now
spares us from redoubling it,
our next time around—otherwise,
how to explain her focus on the words
Tony sang, of eagerness for what's next—
how he could barely wait.

Approaching Candles in the Dark

Warm air arrives through the vents,
just as I felt a little chill, on my skin
and my heart beats faster, in excitement.
This is the Swedish festival of lights,
called St. Lucia Day, named for a Sicilian saint.
She gave her dowry to the poor, and for that,
she was run through, with a sword.
Ever after, the girl who portrays her, wears
a long white dress, with a red sash at her waist,
and evergreen as a crown, lit with candles.
The oldest daughter, brings her family breakfast
before dawn—coffee and special buns.
She arrives, lighting the darkness, saying:
St. Lucia invites you to breakfast.

I learned of the tradition through a historic doll—
a picture of the girl in costume, on the cover of a book.
I gave it all to my daughter—the doll, the books,
an outfit for her—we reenacted the tradition,
that I was never taught, as the oldest daughter
growing up, with two Swedish American parents.
I teased my mother—why didn't I get to do that?
They were assimilated—Mom refused to learn the language,
when she was growing up—no matter—
we had our fun, and somewhere, I have photographs
of my girl, with her Swedish name, Kaja, walking down
a long dark hall, wearing a battery operated crown,
with a tray of my Christmas cookies, and coffee
for me and her father—this is that morning. So,
I will leave a plate of cookies for you, when I go walking.

Chagall Kiss Cup

I forgot to use my Sunday coffee cup,
I noticed, after I was done—
just a ritual, I like—it has a detail
of a painting by Chagall—a couple
in a mid-air kiss, as she holds a bouquet—
a surreal glimpse of them—it was my daughter's.

When I realized yesterday, that I had forgotten,
I thought, I can drink from it tomorrow—
I can regain the lost magic, that rubs off
from my connection to her, through her objects,
like her pencils that I use here, every morning,
to collaborate with my subconscious.

There is a vast, universal pool—the collective,
that we all have access to, through our own piece of it—
a gateway can open—so, I sip from my Chagall kiss cup,
as I call it, on another day of the week.
I sip expectantly, in the quiet darkness,
with blueness at the horizon to the East, just starting.

Mornings here are December cold, so the heat
from the furnace cycles on, and I circle back
to the cup—the talisman I had forgotten, now reclaimed.
I remind myself, nothing is lost, in the grander scheme.
What would my girl say, about my seasonal concerns?
Holidays will happen—I don't need to be collateral damage.

Face to Face

I remember saying to my friend,
love is all there is.
It's what we have, or can have
that is real.
I remember First Corinthians 13
What attaches us,
connects me to you
and you to me,
interlocking links.
It is what lasts
beyond even the chasm,
that is death.
I testify to its resilience,
not just tragic,
but a comfort—
revelation hidden
at first, in the pain of loss.
Each experience
indelible,
what life can give us—
and this path
to the infinite.

Coffee Stains

A drop of coffee slipped down the side of my cup
I dug in my pocket for a tissue to blot it up
but it had dried there—a temporary stain
like a tear that escapes the eye, and stings my cheek.
A scar for a while, disrupting a placid day
with feelings—the intrusion of memory—

Loss barges in, like an uninvited guest at a party.
It doesn't seem to know its place, or arrive at my convenience,
like the way truth gets blurted out, when I'm trying to work.
No social structure is really immune, from being dismantled
by a wailing tune, expressing what needs to be communicated—
at the end of the rope, there is nothing to do but fall.

I land here with a thump, and survey my bruises
and the state of my heart—there is pain
alongside fresh disappointment, that facts haven't changed.
There is no happy ending to take the place of what happened;
that it's just not acceptable, carries no weight—
the past is implacable, unmoved, like stars in outer space.

What is one person, anyway—I gather my bones
and rise from the ground—nothing gets you out of duties,
like the paper that is due tomorrow in class, or the tax bill.
Mistakes will be made, and have their consequences.
The enterprise continues on its way through time.
I am left to try again, to show, what it all felt like.

Some Visitations

A note arrived in my mailbox
from a friend of my daughter's
now living out of state,
just to let me know she's been thinking of her
on the approach of her 40th birthday.

She asked if she was correct—
was the math right? She was a younger friend.
Now, a grown woman with two sons,
and as a Mom, she said she feels for me in my loss.

On the same day, as we walked in the arroyo
below the museums, on what they call Museum Hill,
a black winged butterfly flew over and towards me—
black with white along the outer edges, first one
of the season that has not yet begun, though it's warmer—

Hello! I exclaimed out loud, and stopped to watch
its dancing flight—first one, I told you.
We saw it again in the same stretch, walking home.
I smiled, feeling that my daughter visited us.
Then, I took in the love for her, shared in the letter.

Her friend is now a therapist for young women;
she speaks of her to clients, so vividly recalled—
how she embraced her contradictions, and how
"she turned her quirks, into her superpowers"—
that my daughter grew back for me, in dimension.
I thank her for sharing, the vision she has kept of her.

The Girl in the Grave

I'm in a swirling world of change
like in a tornado—things are rearranged
after being upended and torn apart.
I have a hard time accepting what I have chosen.
Again, my body registers, and mirrors disruption.

Logical timing in the real world of work
ran up against the emotional calendar—
as if it didn't matter, the birthday of my daughter,
although she isn't here anymore, to honor—
as if I didn't notice she would have been forty.

Plans are always subject to adjustment.
You pay it back, if you didn't pay in advance.
The heart lets you know what it needs—
one way or another, finds the valve for relief.
We brought her flowers, though the cemetery lost trees.

Jet said, it was shocking, and it did look bleak.
Stacked up wood and stumps replacing live trees,
which clearly had died, by the look of the remains.
All too congruent with the purpose of the place—
but we were preoccupied with the girl in the grave.

And in its wake, my body was sickened
seemingly out of the blue—unexpected and rude.
It was all too much, and I had to stop—
I had to pay attention to recovery, to the exclusion
of all else—even support I had scheduled.

We do what we can, with what happens in life.
My first day of retirement was spent sick in bed,
accompanied by worries I couldn't go on my trip—
it's been more of a roller coaster than I imagined,
but it seems I'll survive, to fly off, to adventure.

Guiding Lights

I saw the Full Moon
lit pink in the Western sky
when I got up late for me,
before it slipped out of sight
and sank to its bed.
I know how it feels to be spent,
after great efforts.
An hour later, I see the Sun
It seems too bright
as I look East towards the spot
where it reaches through trees—
I blink, still gauzy headed
swimming up to some surface
from overdue rest,
and remembrance of what isn't
anymore in this world.
Not yet reoriented,
knowing there's a coming storm.
I continue processing
from a new point
on the spiral of life,
what has gone before me,
what it means
to lose the future
of her substance and form.
Tender is the consciousness
where all but love vanishes
yet fiercely shines on—
her spirit, through this song.

Becoming a Healer

As soon as her boyfriend said, back in the winter,
every seventeen years, the calendar is identical—
the dates fall on the same days of the week, that is—
my brain leaped forward to today.
May 27th would come on a Sunday.
I knew this because he said, he was reusing
a calendar from 2001, the year she died.

And now we have come to the date
Soon it will be the time, around 8:30 a.m.
I don't have to re-live each moment,
although in my mind, I just did.
It's hard to know where to focus,
on her life, or her demise—it all comes back,
whatever would be wisest—and just now,
I can't help but notice a convention of crows.
Their voices are loud, as they call out—

Perhaps they are protecting a nest
with a young one—people are advised
to stay far from their nests, just as we're told
not to come between a bear and her cub—
I would have fought off Death,
but I didn't know how—that's the ultimate
predator, and while the doctors tried
to intervene on a cellular level,
they didn't succeed, and so, she died.

And really, where do we go from there?
It's never been clear—I've never understood
what to do, in response—I've gnashed my teeth
and torn my hair, so to speak, to no avail.
In the short term, I knew I had another child to raise
and that got me through—my life had a purpose
in practical terms, and loss of faith
had to wait for another day to consider.
Gradually—though I hate to say it—it returned,
and while it feels like betrayal, healing has occurred.

Her Bag of Tricks

I tingle with sensations
but know how to calm myself,
by taking slow breaths—
muscles learn, how to relax.
They become extended, not clenched
like a fist, nor constricted in a cramp.

The morning has quieted—
Somewhere, a baby sleeps after restlessness.
I push hair back off my cheek
from tickling irritation. One bird calls.
It pauses in between. Then, a crow
repeats, its loud caw-caw-caw.

Sky is white, but trees hold the darkness
a little longer, and delay night's surrender.
My days look different now
although I am remembering how to dress
in nicer clothes, despite the fact
I have left the work force.

I am in a reorientation process,
with only the stars to guide me.
Warmed by an inner light,
I move forward with a sense of myself,
where I am growing open again—not defined,
but informed, by the past.

Like the vision I have of my daughter
as a babysitter, who came with a bag
of tricks to assignments—books and games
puzzles and dolls, perhaps—paper and colored sticks,
for drawing—that is how I bring history into today,
like life to a party—and, may her smile inspire me.

My Private Muse

I prepare myself like the fertile ground in Spring,
turning the soil over, welcoming rain—even snow
that came, all mixed up in showers, yesterday.
We got in a short walk between them, later
in the afternoon than usual. Things are changing
out there, and inside myself, as I begin to shape
a collection that is located close to my heart.

That is an area where doctors hesitate to operate
It's delicate, like the brain, which is also implicated—
my most vital organs, and as a result, I am careful
and hesitant—I will go slowly, and notice my emotions.
How they show up in my body, if they register as pain—
I will be quick to listen, to what messages arrive
and take roost—I will make adjustments, for my truth.

Luckily, as I work, I'll have an angel at my side.
Like a large, swooping crow, I will hear a loud cawing
in the sky overhead, repeating itself, if I ignore a message.
Or, I'll be kissed by the sight of an early butterfly, if I'm
attuned to the wavelength of her spirit, visiting inside—
where our truths mingle, in harmony and are aligned.
It will become the nexus for my words, to be presented.

I sense the time is right, to reveal my perspective
in the hope, perhaps in vain, that I can do it justice.
She will be there, helping me select, what best conveys
the ineffable—the grace in the heart of this mother
who finds I have been rearranged, by what is unspeakable.
And yet, must be described, in melody and pictures—
her memory—magnetically attractive, and, undeniable.

As If I Could Fly

Winds bring disruption, sway the shadows
made by Sun's early rays, as it tops the foothills
and kick starts another day—winds portend change.

I wished to be free of a work place, after I exited
and now, it has ceased to exist—an example of watching
what you wish for, as something in there is a powerful truth.

The weather is unsettled, and the energy stirred up
can take us far—I have pointed my arrow to a project
that has incubated for years, as I gained perspective.

I reviewed some explorations of my anguish,
and realized I don't want to include them in work
I am gathering for a small collection, on a sore subject.

It's as if I have grown wings, and flown high above
the grounding Earth, with its gravity pulling me down.
What I want to show is from a different angle, perched

like a bird in a high tree top, that calls or sings
obnoxious or sweet sounding—how is it I'm able
to land in unusual spots, for a person who knows

what I have found out, through the distractions of
daily living—of working at a job, and falling in love.
Then, building a new partnership—through illness

through other forms of strife—I see her everywhere,
in my heart, in the loud crows, and butterflies which
are silent, as beauty often is—I feel her when I'm hopeful.

Somehow, her spirit lives, and travels on Spring winds.
I recognize her guidance, as I undertake describing life
after her body died—I'm lifted, as my tears fall, and then dry.

Night Vision

I turned and saw my daughter smiling,
standing in my dream—younger and healthy,
looking as she did in the photo we used
for her obituary—in this way, she has appeared
in other dreams, and made me happy.
Then she vanishes—my son said, he has seen her
in his dreams too, as if she hadn't died, after all
filling him with happiness—then, she is gone.

This time I also saw a photograph, briefly
and understood she had been pictured in it
Then it was gone, too, and the scene dissolved.
To both of us, it feels like an opportunity lost
Did she come to tell us something—what
wisdom or information did we miss?
So near, yet so far. My dream devolved
into a cleaning project that never got done—
the mess kept coming, until I woke up.

Sky was lavender, and now it is white with clouds.
I was hopeful earlier, I would see the moon rise.
The newspaper said, it would be around 6:30—
up and over the foothills, sometime later, but alas
clouds fill the sky to the east. I was briefly
brushed with divinity as I slept, touched
by the love that beats strongly on, and visits
in this gracious way every so often—before we drop
back down, to the Earth's solid ground.

FINALE

Roll the Credits

I saw the name of Kaja
scrolling down my TV screen,
one of the people who works there,
every day behind the scenes.
Just a nanosecond
as I kept watching the screen,
after the program ended—
and it leaped out at me.
Did I even see it?
Honey, thanks for visiting.

Christine R. Lund is a poet and writer living in Santa Fe, New Mexico, with her husband, Neil C. Trager. Neil is a photographer, and founding director of the Samuel Dorsky Museum of Art, now retired. They are collaborating on two books of poems and photographs. ME AND HER SHADOW is Christine's first published chapbook of poems. She has written two novels, several chapbooks, and writes every day before dawn. In the last few years, she compiled three full length collections of poetry. Her poetry has been published in *The Denver Post*, *The Hungry Poet's Cookbook* and *The New Poets' Anthology*, among other publications. Her travel articles and book reviews have appeared in *The New York Times*, *The Albuquerque Journal* and *Endless Vacation* magazine. She received a Bachelor of Arts degree from Boston University, with a major in English literature.

ME AND HER SHADOW is a collection of poems in honor of her daughter, Kaja Mauldin (Kaja is pronounced kai-ya). Kaja's father was the Pulitzer Prize winning political cartoonist and author, Bill Mauldin. He is best known for his cartoons during World War II of two foot soldiers, Willie and Joe. He and Christine also have a son, Sam Mauldin.

A talented young artist herself, Kaja unfortunately was diagnosed with cancer and died shortly after she turned 23. One of Kaja's self-portraits appears on the cover of ME AND HER SHADOW. This collection both celebrates her life, and tells the story of Christine's journey of healing, over the course of 18 years following Kaja's death. It is shaped as a musical drama, with poems taking the place of songs. Christine states, "I offer this chapbook of poems in the spirit of love, with hopes it may help others who have experienced the loss of a loved one—especially a child." She has just completed a fourth full length collection of poems, on the theme of possibilities available to women in the third phase of their lives, one of her collaborations with her husband, Neil.

www.ingramcontent.com/pod-product-compliance
Lightning Source LLC
LaVergne TN
LVHW041556070426
835507LV00011B/1110